GO AND BE SUCCESSFUL

WES BEAVIS

D1382517

This book contains the personal opinions and ideas of the author. It is not intended to be a substitute for gaining specific professional advice from legal, tax, investment, accounting, insurance, or financial advisors. It is the reader's responsibility to consult professional advice or services with regard to any strategies outlined in this book and to determine their relevance to the reader's geographical location and personal situation. The contents of this book in no way dilute the absolute responsibility of the reader to perform due diligence with regard to any transactions nor do they absolve the reader from, or assign to the author or publisher, responsibility for the consequences of any actions taken.

Go and Be Successful
by Wes Beavis

Copyright © 2008 W. J. Beavis

MANUFACTURED IN THE UNITED STATES OF AMERICA BY
Birmingham Press - San Diego, California USA 92121

10 9 8 7 6 5 4 3 2

For information about special discounts for quantity orders please contact POWERBORN by going to:
www.WesBeavis.com or calling 1-877-Wes-Book

COPYRIGHT & PUBLISHING ADMINISTRATION
POWERBORN - Irvine, California USA 92602
www.WesBeavis.com

COVER DESIGN BY PlainJoeStudios.com
COVER PHOTOGRAPH BY Samuel Lippke

Library of Congress Cataloging-in-Publication Data

Beavis, Wesley James.
Go and Be Successful: directions for those who want to get there /
Wes Beavis   p.   cm.
1. Success in business– United States.   2. Quality of life– United States.   3. Work & Family– United States.   4. Self-actualization / Maturation (Psychology)
I. Title   158.1 BEA —dc20   2008
ISBN-13: 978-1-888741-08-7
ISBN-10: 1-888741-08-2

To my grandfather
Reginald Hector Beavis
who lived and conducted business with
inspiring faith and integrity

Also by the Author

Become the Person You Dream of Being
Dating the Dream
Escape to Prosperity
Give Your Life a Success Makeover

Contents

Introduction

If you had to choose between love or money, go with love. Better to have love and be poor. Not as good to be rich and have no love. But after many years on the road of life, I have come to this conclusion: Ultimately, it is better to have love *and* be rich. With much abundance. In that order.

While you can succeed in many areas that can't be tallied on the financial score board, this book *Go and Be Successful*, has an emphasis on succeeding financially. All of the topics are included because they influence the bottom line. I am not endorsing 'capitalism myopia'—that financial success is everything. Indeed there's more to life than money. Some have proven that it's possible to live a noble life without having money. Yet, I am compelled by the reality that more can be done with money than without it. More good. More life. For all.

So I write with enthusiasm. It's better for you to love *and* be rich than otherwise. True gain does not come at someone's loss. Raising your financial tide will elevate more boats than just yours. It is possible for you to be successful. No law against it. All you need, in addition to the potential that you already have, is some encouragement and guidance. To this end I have written for you, *Go and Be Successful.*

—Wes Beavis

1

Decide to Be Successful

Entry to a foreign country requires a visa. Driving on public roads requires a license. Adding a room to your home requires a permit from the city. There are many things for which you need permission to proceed. Similarly, you need authorization to be successful. You cannot begin to succeed without it. You need consent from the person who is in charge of your life in order to be successful. Who controls your life? It should be you. You control the permits department. If you have given away your authority, it's time to get it back. Because the first step towards success is self-authorization.

Strangely, many people wish they could be successful but they don't give themselves permission to be so. In their heart of hearts, they think the abundant life is for others not them. When they enter the airplane of life they automatically turn to the right towards economy class.

Subconsciously, they think First Class is for others. Most never write themselves a permission slip to share in the abundance.

We succeed only as far as we permit ourselves. The level to which we rise is often only as high as what we allow. In essence, we regulate our position in life according to whatever license we have been given, either by ourselves, others or our circumstances. We can dream and wish all we like but we will stay where we're at, until we issue ourselves with a travel visa to go beyond it.

You have the authority to pursue a better life. Use your authority! Ordain yourself to be successful. You are just as worthy of succeeding as anyone else. Deciding to be successful starts with giving yourself permission to live an abundant life. Do it now. Look at yourself in the mirror and say, "I have every right to be successful. I give myself permission to live life at an abundant level."

Just as your current life is the result of your choices, your future will be determined by your choices. If you are frustrated, unfulfilled or envious, the answer lies not in hoping for a change in circumstances but in exercising your power to make decisions. The way out of a lousy circumstance will always come by way of making a decision. Troubles can not lock you into any situation that can't be improved by decision making.

Too many people surrender control of their lives to other people or prevailing conditions. They complain that life is not going their way. They're unhappy about their expectations not being met. They start blaming things for their misfortune as if blame is the way to usher in a favorable change. Frankly, if blaming was effective I would know. Through much use I have earned a Ph.D. in blaming! Yet, such expertise has never improved my conditions one bit.

Admittedly, the deck of life may have dealt you some tough cards. You may have every right to blame something else for the difficulties which you bear. But it is useless to exercise that right. For as long as you blame someone or something else for the condition of your life, you put your future in shackles. This is why. If you blame outside forces for your condition, you will be inclined to think that outside forces have to change before you can experience improvement in your life. You live at the mercy of outside forces. That's why you are shackled.

When you have the courage to concede, "My life is the result of my decisions" you remove the shackles and empower your future. You empower it because you realize that YOU are in control of your life with your decision making power. You are not at the mercy of other people or circumstances however imposing they may be. If you haven't surrendered your decision making to them, they are still subservient to your decision making.

Most things do not work out as planned. If you are young and starting out in life, it won't be long before you learn this. If you are longing to start over, it is because your previous plan has fallen to pieces. No one escapes those challenging times when life chips away at your plans with all the grace of a jackhammer. To add more humiliation to broken dreams, we live in a world that loudly celebrates and gives media attention to a plan that becomes a runaway success. Too easily we are seduced into thinking that there are two types of people: those who are born to succeed, and those who are born to admire those who succeed. So if our plans fall in a heap, it's too tempting to resign ourselves to the latter group. We decide to be content with what we have. In doing so, we decide to be average.

Life is NOT over when things don't work out as planned. If you have a bag full of broken plans, you are normal! You still have the right to be successful. No one can take that right away from you. The right to be successful is only lost when you surrender it to outside forces. Regardless of what may have happened to you or not happened to you, a course correction is still your decision. Adjusting your plans is up to you. Creating a better future is your decision.

Your life is the result of your decisions. You have the license to make them. If your decisions are good ones, they will position you for good outcomes. You are not at the mercy of someone else's benevolence or even the right conditions. You have the ultimate influence over your future prospects. Decide to be successful. It's your choice.

Putting the Principle to Work

1. I hereby retire the following people and/or situations from determining the quality of my future:

_____

_____

_____

_____

_____

2. I, _____, accept full responsibility that my current position in life is the result of my decisions and I no longer hold anyone else responsible.

3. As of this date, _____, I appoint myself as Managing Director of my life and reserve the right to make all decisions necessary to improve my future.

4. I decide to be successful. Some of the fruits of that success will be:

_____

_____

_____

_____

_____

2

Think to Win

Rachel Scott lost her life in the infamous Columbine High School massacre. Years later, her brother was interviewed on the Oprah show. He had ample invitation to comment on the deeds of the ill-famed perpetrators. But he chose not to, simply saying, "What you give your attention to, you give power to." Quite possibly, they are the ten most potent words in this book. Indeed, whatever gets your focus gets magnified.

The quality of our life is determined by the quality of our decisions and the quality of our decisions is determined by the quality of our thinking. So what you think about is a persuasive force. You give power to that which you give your attention. This principle works equally well to your benefit or your detriment. Your life will follow your thoughts. A good life is the result of good thinking. If you want to win in life, the process starts with developing great patterns of thought.

I'm not sure if I grew up in poverty but it sure felt like it. New clothes for my siblings and I meant either a trip to the thrift store, being given 'hand-me-downs' by other families, or my dear mother creating something with her trustworthy Elna sewing machine. My dad raised chickens to help feed us. The chicken feed came in soft cotton bags. My mother would unpick the seams of the cotton bags and sew several together to make bed sheets out of them. Since real bed sheets were expensive to buy, my siblings and I would compete with each other to get the latest 'chicken feed bed sheet' that mother would create. That Elna sewing machine was always making something. It was worth its weight in gold in the way it helped our family get by financially.

From time to time, my mother would want a new dress. But a new dress for her meant buying some dress material and a pattern. The pattern would be a collection of tissue paper shapes neatly folded into an envelope. On the front of the envelope, there would be a picture of what the dress should look like once finished. Mother would lay the paper patterns on the material and cut the material to the shape of the paper patterns. Then all the pieces of material would be sewn together to create the dress. If mother wanted a new dress, she would buy a new pattern to help her create it.

Our minds work the same. Over our lives, we acquire mental patterns that influence the way we divide our thoughts, just as a paper dress pattern forms the basis of how new material is divided. Some of these mental patterns we get from our parents, others we obtain from past experiences, while other patterns of thought we blindly accept from other people's opinions. The bottom line is that these patterns are powerful. All new thoughts are mentally processed according to our pre-existing mental patterns.

One of the subconscious mental patterns that formed from my childhood experiences was that large families and financial scarcity go together. Hence, any positive ideas about having a large brood didn't make it past my well-established mental pattern that large families and financial scarcity go together.

It's not enough to say 'think better'. All the positive thinking in the world may not be enough to overcome your existing mental patterns. Thinking better will require you to evaluate and eject some erroneous mental patterns that you have collected over the years.

Here's another example. Having trouble forgiving someone who has wronged you comes from an erroneous mental pattern. It comes from a pattern that mandates that the perpetrator must at least be sorry for what they have done in order to earn your forgiveness. It could be expressed this way, "Until they apologize for what they've done, they don't deserve my forgiveness!" Such a thought comes from a faulty mental pattern.

The right mental pattern is to understand that forgiveness is all about your freedom. When someone has wronged you, forgiveness is your conquering weapon against the influence that wrong can have upon you. If you don't forgive, then you will naturally stew on the offense, not realizing that the more you stew upon it; the more power you are giving it. Stewing on the offense keeps it alive. Forgiveness stops the offense dead in its tracks from having further influence over you. If you have trouble forgiving someone, it's not about how much you have been wronged but how much you have the wrong mental pattern.

You may drink from a steady stream of positive thoughts but still remain dehydrated of personal power because your subconscious mental patterns are cracked. All the positive thoughts in the world won't help you if your existing mental patterns keep tossing them out of your mind.

The right to control what you think about will always be yours. If you are thinking about negative things or have limiting mental patterns, it's because you have given yourself permission for that to happen. Your thought life is your responsibility. Circumstances can provide many opportunities to think negatively but they can't make you think negative thoughts. If you find yourself mulling over weakening thoughts, you have allowed such. If you are not living the life that you want, start by challenging your personal mental patterns. If my mother wanted a different dress she would go and buy a new pattern. Getting a new life will require you to acquire a new mental pattern or two.

A better life always starts with better thinking. It is impossible to move in a positive direction whilst being governed by negative thoughts and patterns. Program your head with thoughts and patterns that empower positive advancement. The quality of your future is determined by what gets your mental attention today. Think to win.

Putting the Principle to Work

I suspect the following mental patterns of mine are faulty:

_____

_____

_____

_____

This *faulty* thought pattern_____

_____

is hereby replaced with this *success* thought pattern

_____

This *faulty* thought pattern_____

_____

is hereby replaced with this *success* thought pattern

_____

This *faulty* thought pattern_____

_____

is hereby replaced with this *success* thought pattern

_____

Write the new thought patterns on a card and carry them with you. Refer to them several times during the day.

3

Make Use of Dream Power

A dream has a mysterious power to propel a man beyond his abilities. If you consider yourself average but have a vision for an above average life, that vision will draw you upwards. Having a dream is integral to personal advancement. Better to have a dream and no resources than have an abundance of resources and no vision for their use.

It takes more than a dream to succeed. Yet, it's harder to succeed without one. The right dream in the right heart can boost a person to levels way beyond what you would expect for their talent and skills. A dream does not negate the value of knowledge, skills, and talent. But having a dream is what ignites all those qualities. A dream gives you a hunger to leverage them and develop them to your advantage.

Everyone is primed with an imagination. You are meant to dream. Your capacity for imagination is there so that you can cultivate a dream that motivates you. In life, you will always achieve more when you hold an image of something that you would like to see become reality.

A dream can form in many ways. Sometimes you see something in another person that inspires you to strive for the same. Other times, a dream can arise from desperate experiences.

When my father died, I was twenty-four years old and my younger brother was twenty-two. Since dad had died at the age of fifty, we were thrust into responsibilities for which we had not been prepared. One of the things we had to do was to visit the bank that held the mortgage on our parents' home. My brother and I wanted to find out the condition of dad's financial affairs. In such a time of despair, we wanted to comfort our grieving mother with the knowledge that at least she would keep the roof over her head.

The bank manager ushered my brother and me into his office and gave us his condolences. Then he opened up my parents' bank file and began to explain the gravity of the situation. My folks had taken out a mortgage to buy the home just a few years earlier. We were hoping that there was an associated insurance coverage to pay off the mortgage in the event of something like this happening. Alas, there was no such cover. The bank manager reluctantly sent us on our way with the knowledge that the mortgage was still owed and the current month's payment was due. The heaviness of my heart as we left his office was immense. How were we to tell our mother, who had just lost her husband, that losing the family home was a real possibility?

It was a dark time. Often dark times provide just the right conditions for the birth of a powerful dream. For me, the tragic experience of losing my dad and having the security of the family home put in jeopardy, set a dream into motion. What would it be like to buy a home and pay off the mortgage? Was it possible to actually own a home free and clear of any mortgage? I determined that it was possible and set about making the dream come true.

You will be more energized with a dream than without one. What may seem an impossible task becomes possible with the assistance of dream power. In my case, the onerous undertaking of paying off a home mortgage became an invigorating game. The dream of making my last mortgage payment inspired me to achieve increased sales. Every extra dollar earned was paid off the mortgage. It was motivating to see the payoff date creep forward with every extra effort. It felt great to make the final payment. Dream power works!

Some people have no shortage of personal dreams. The dreams just pop into their heart without effort. Others have to cultivate a dream. Instead of waiting for one to come to you, go out and find one. Give yourself permission to dream. Maybe your imagination has been buried under a load of responsibilities. Be assured that if you spend some time cultivating a dream, your dream will strengthen you for all your responsibilities. A dream will invigorate you. It will give you passion to get up and get at it. In fact, if you are struggling to get up, it is quite possible that you have nothing in your life that is inspiring you to get up.

If you haven't got an exciting dream, it doesn't mean that you're not capable of having one. It just means that you have to be more proactive. Venture out beyond your normal routine. Expand your social circle. Gain more exposure to the wonders that the world has to offer. Meet more interesting people. The initial steps on your success path must include capturing a dream that fuels your enthusiasm. Dreams are out there. Find one, put it in your heart and let its empowering effect elevate your life.

If you have a dream of paying off your home mortgage or any other debt, use the Motivator Calculator™ on my website www.WesBeavis.com. See the powerful effect that extra payments can have in bringing forward your Debt-Freedom Day!

Putting the Principle to Work

Write down three dreams in your life that have come true:

1. _____

2. _____

3. _____

What are your current dreams?

_____

_____

_____

_____

_____

_____

I have shared my dream with the following people who encourage me to keep going for it:

_____

_____

_____

_____

4

Compare Yourself to Others

One of the greatest temptations within humanity is the temptation to compare ourselves to each other. We just naturally do it. We are drawn to do a quick mental measurement to see how we stack up to those around us. Perhaps it is our insecurities that drive us to do it. We compare hoping that we will measure up, or even better, discover that we exceed the person to whom we measure ourselves. If we measure up, we somehow feel better about ourselves. If we fall short, that's another story!

Is playing the comparison game healthy? Should we stop playing it? Is it possible to stop? The reality is that we have been comparing for so long, it is too hard a habit to break. So rather than beat ourselves up over it, let's continue to get out the mental measuring tape. Let's compare away but do so in a productive way.

One of the challenges about comparing is that we tend to compare ourselves on our worst day to someone having his or her best day. It's not a rational comparison nor a fair one. So should we halt that practice? Absolutely not. Keep on comparing. It can still provide you with motivation to improve your game.

Comparing yourself to someone successful can prod you out of your languishing stupor—if you let it. Comparing yourself to someone successful can demoralize you into a spiral of depression—if you let it. Here's the point. It's inevitable that you will compare yourself with others. But what you let the comparison do to you is your choice. The person that you're comparing yourself to is not responsible for how you feel afterwards. So after all the comparing is said and done, you alone are responsible for the outcome. What have you let it do to you? Inspire you or depress you? The choice is yours.

It's true that dangers accompany the practice of comparing ourselves with others. There will always be those who are worse than you, which can lead you to be prideful. There will always be those who are better than you, which can lead you to be discouraged. Popular opinion says, "Therefore, don't compare." But reality proves that we do anyway. So, go ahead and compare your life to others but approach it in the right way. If you catch yourself getting depressed, prideful or discouraged then you're not doing it right. Make the performance of others inspire you to improve yourself.

Putting the Principle to Work

1. I select the following person to compare my performance to:

_____

2. I, _____, accept full responsibility for making sure the outcome of the comparison inspires personal improvement and does not lead to discouragement, depression or pride.

3. I will compare the following (scale 1 to 10):

My vehicle _____Their vehicle_____

The quality of how I dress _____
The quality of how they dress _____

The condition of my home _____
The condition of their home _____

My income _____ Their income _____

My ongoing education plan _____
Their ongoing education plan _____

How many hours I work _____
How many hours they work _____

5

Determine the Best Use
of You

You can do just about anything you want to in life. But that doesn't mean you should do anything you want. If your desire is to succeed, then go and do what you are good at doing. If you are a person with any ambition, you won't have a shortage on 'ideas' that could make you successful. But you will always be more successful with ideas that orbit around your talents.

Your destiny is written upon your talents and natural abilities. Initially, it's not about being the best in the world at something. It's about doing what you are best at doing. Do what produces the most positive results. Get this right and you increase your chances of succeeding, enjoying yourself, and maybe even being the best in the world at it.

Billionaire Warren Buffett summarized why he successfully invested two hundred and ninety million dollars in a certain company stating, "They stick with what they understand and let their abilities, not their egos, determine what they attempt."

Too many people allow their egos to keep them doggedly pursuing something that has, after reasonable efforts, produced minimal results. For example, it is admirable for someone to chase his dream of becoming a professional musician. But it is unwise to spend years trying to 'make it' with nothing to show for it but an empty bank account and a receding hairline. Warren Buffett has significant ability in playing the ukulele. But his stock holders are glad he focused on something other than a music career!

Be diligent in trying your hand and putting your mind to different things. Explore your inclinations and develop burgeoning abilities. In the pursuit of discovering what you should do, Dr. Phil McGraw counsels people to "kiss as many frogs as you can and go with the one that turns into a prince." But I would add to that by saying, there comes a time when you have to make a decision. You can't kiss frogs for a living. There comes a time when it's best to go with the frog that most resembles a prince; the one that gives you the best return for your efforts.

If you are a lamp, put yourself on the lamp stand which allows you to cast the most light, regardless of the shape of the lamp stand. It is better to be on a rusty lamp stand and radiate brilliantly, than to be on a golden stand barely throwing out a noticeable lumen. Confidence comes when you see positive results for your efforts. The results easily compensate for the modesty of whatever you are standing upon in order to achieve those results. Being successful is about amassing positive outcomes, not about the image or prestige of what you do to get those outcomes. Positive results bring confidence and confidence attracts success and the cycle perpetuates.

The greater your results, the greater your impact and the more the doors of opportunity will open up to you. So ask yourself, what is the best use of me? Of all the things I have tried up to now, what has produced the greatest results? Yes, be motivated by your dreams and hope to do something that you love, but don't get yourself lost and empty-handed hunting for the elusive golden goose. The way forward is to ride the ability that produces the most positive results. Identify that ability, stick with it and increase it.

Putting the Principle to Work

Over my life I have taken the following possibilities for a test drive:

_____

_____

_____

_____

_____

_____

Of all the things I have tried up to this point, what focus has produced the greatest results?

_____

_____

_____

When I am engaged in the following activities I feel like I am effectively brightening the room:

_____

_____

_____

_____

_____

6

Position Yourself to Succeed

"I just happened to be in the right place at the right time!" This is the recurring testimony made by numerous successful people. Many attest to 'luck' playing a key role in their breaking through to success. So how much should you rely upon luck as part of your success plan?

Don't factor luck in at all. You can succeed without ever being lucky. Put your energy into positioning yourself well. Put yourself in the right place to be noticed by the right people on the right occasion. Doors of opportunity will start to open as a result of you doing so. When those doors open, some will say that you're lucky. But luck came by way of you being strategic.

A few years ago, my wife and I met three teenage sisters who had formed a singing group. They sang for our organization and we provided them hospitality in our home for a few days. They were sweet kids and easy to encourage. They were welcomed to stay for much longer.

And indeed they would have received from us lots of love, encouragement and free accommodation! Instead, they traveled to a talent camp in Colorado. There they subjected themselves to the possible humiliation of people being ambivalent towards their singing efforts.

How did they fare? They have gone on to become one of the most popular female bands in America. While they could have stayed with us and received a regular feeding of love and encouragement, we couldn't have given them a recording contract—no matter how much we loved on them.

Positioning yourself to succeed means leaving the love nest. It is so easy to hang around the people who are going build you up and keep you comfortable. Many do and wonder why life isn't getting any better for them. You can't make headway by staying around your fan club. At some point you have to go out and subject yourself to the possibility of getting your teeth kicked in by the realities of the marketplace.

The three sisters traveled to a place where there were representatives from the music industry. In doing so, they positioned themselves for the possibility of two things: rejection or breakthrough. They were willing to swallow their pride if they weren't well received. But they also stacked the odds in their favor by having prepared a good foot to put forward. It's essential for you to do the same.

Before you venture out, have your skill developed the best you can. Know all that you can about your field or product. And when you present yourself, do so to the right people. If you can't get to the right people, then 'sing' for the wrong people for experience's sake. But don't be dismayed when the wrong audience does not offer you a deal or provide you with a sale. Consider it good experience and don't let their ambivalence demoralize you. Too many people give up as a result of demonstrating to the wrong demographic.

Early in my speaking career, I was invited to speak to a foreign audience. The entire program was spoken in a language not my own. Even with the help of interpreters, I could tell that I was not connecting with them. At the conclusion of the program, I had one sale. The person who had arranged for me to come and speak made a purchase. It was a mercy sale, so that didn't count as a real sale! As I drove home on the 101 Freeway in Los Angeles, I felt low enough to quit.

Three months later, I was driving home along the same stretch of the 101 Freeway. I had just finished another speaking engagement. After one presentation, my sales amounted to a career high. Total sales were in excess of the price of my first home!

What had changed in the three months between the two events? Simply the audience. I had delivered with equal passion in both scenarios. Both had access to the same products. I think I may have even worn the same suit on both occasions. The difference was the audience.

Too many people give up not because they lacked

ability, nor because they had a bad product. They give up because they pitched themselves to the wrong people. No matter how good your aim, aiming at the wrong target is setting yourself up for failure. Discern the audience most likely to respond with the results you want. Position yourself for success by getting out there and pitching yourself to the right people.

SOW YOUR SEEDS

Sow your seeds wherever you go
For you never know where they'll grow;
Some will sit, some will flop
Some of your seeds will grow into a crop.

You're never quite sure when your seed comes to rest
Whether the soil is bad, or simply the best;
Just sow everywhere 'cause the truth be told
Some seeds will produce a hundred-fold.

And as seasons pass full of your toil,
You'll get to know the better soil;
The places best for most your grains
Are the fields that yield your greatest gains.

—Wes Beavis

Putting the Principle to Work

I have received the best response from the following target group/s:

_____

_____

_____

_____

I have received the worst response from those who are:

_____

_____

_____

_____

On the basis of the above, my energies are better spent being directed towards the following prospects:

_____

_____

_____

_____

7

Seek Out Inspiring People

Other people shape you. It is a fact most clearly proven by young people. We call it peer group pressure. It is that powerful force that causes a young person to conform to resemble their peers. Guess what? The power of peer group pressure doesn't go away with age. You will naturally become like the people with whom you associate, whether you are fourteen or fifty-four.

People are amazingly influential. Who you mix with matters. You can be taking on the characteristics of people around you without realizing it. So be responsible and show some discernment in choosing the people with whom you associate. The best way to control how other people influence you is to select with whom you spend your time.

This is not an endorsement to be elitist or to develop a sense of superiority over others. Just realize the power that relationships have on who you are and what you become. Remember the adage, "If you lay down with dogs, you'll get up with fleas." The second verse of the same song could be, "If you hang around eagles, you'll learn how to fly." You have to work harder to get to the eagles. They can be more elusive but they can be found if you actively seek them.

The influence of outstanding people will do more to elevate your life than almost anything. If you want to ignite some self-improvement motivation in you, just get into the presence of someone living life at a level you admire. Don't be intimidated or let your insecurity stop you from having great people in your life.

Once, while standing in the customs line at Los Angeles International Airport, I stood behind legendary business philosopher, Jim Rohn. It was a long line and I could have at least said, "Jim, keep writing those awesome books. You have changed my life through your words." But I didn't say anything. I rationalized that he was tired from a long flight and wanted to be left alone. The truth was that I was self-conscious and a big scaredy-cat! My insecurity paid off marvelously with a sizeable dose of regret. Now every time I stand in the customs line in Los Angeles, I look out for legendary Jim Rohn and hope for a second chance!

You don't even need to know great people personally. You can be in their presence without even being known to them. Register for their seminars. Join their professional trade associations. Attend their conferences. Listen to their recorded talks.

I spend most of my time hosting conferences or being away from home speaking at them. Yet, once every three to four months, I attend a conference simply as a delegate. I go as a student to learn and to associate with people who inspire me. Over time, my commitment to attending these conferences has given me the opportunity to become friends with many eagles. Their friendships elevate my attitude and altitude.

Too often seeking out inspiring people gets pushed towards the bottom of the list of things to do. We leave it to when we have some spare time, if and when that ever happens. Create room for inspiring people. Set yourself up to be positively influenced by outstanding people. The bottom line is that if you don't make it a priority, you have only yourself to blame for the fleas!

Putting the Principle to Work

In actively seeking out inspiring people, I put myself at this point on the line:

Poor   Excellent

Two reasons why I'm reluctant to seek out inspiring people:

1. _____

2. _____

The following people have inspired me:

_____

_____

_____

If I could spend an day with any eagle it would be:

_____

I am an eagle to the following people:

_____

_____

Inspiring people I will meet within the next three months:

_____

_____

8

Ask Advice from the Right People

Nobody has lived your life before you. Your life is a brand new journey straight out of the box, unused. If you were a book, you are in the process of being written in real time. So if you are currently writing chapter five of your life, you can't skip over to chapter seven to see how the consequences of your current decisions are going to turn out. Even your parents can't tell you exactly how life is going to unfold for you. Though they are responsible for you being on earth, they can only guide you so much. Most of your journey is for you to figure out the best way you can.

So to get the best out of life, to ensure the story of your life has a happy 'job well done' ending, you have to get a lot of advice along the way. But it has to be good advice as there is no shortage of bad advice. And for good advice, you have to go to the right people.

A fortunate few have parents who have kept life together and succeeded in a balanced way. This is the obvious first port of call in getting good advice. But if your biological parents or grandparents are not in the picture, Robert Kiyosaki has well proven with his *Rich Dad Poor Dad* testimony that you can choose a success dad or mom. And then, why stop there? Find yourself a success brother or sister as well.

Who are the people you admire? Have you ever asked them for their advice? If they are famous, you may not be able to invite them out for a destiny defining dinner. But if they are famous, there's a high likelihood that they have recordings and books from which to glean their advice and guidance.

Success coaches are another great source of gaining good advice. High school athletes have coaches. Professional athletes have coaches. Olympians have coaches. Actors have coaches. So if you want to succeed, wouldn't a success coach make sense? Yet so many 'go it alone' in trying to create a successful life. In reality, for you to get to the end of your days and sing *I Did It My Way*, could be the dumbest admission of your life. Because with some coaching, you could have earned twice as much, gone twice the distance, built twice the equity, had twice the impact, and made half of the mistakes than you would have 'doing it your way!'

It doesn't matter what age or stage you are in life, look for someone to coach you. Actively seek out the right person to assess your position in life. Ask them to help you to create a plan to improve your future. It makes sense to pay them too. People become very willing to pay a counselor to help them recover from their messes. It is a much better investment to pay a coach to steer you away from messing up in the first place.

All of the good advice you need in order to make great decisions is out there. All it takes is some humility and effort on your part to connect with that good advice. Get lots of it. Compare advice with advice then proceed under the influence.

Putting the Principle to Work

The top three advisors in my life to this point have been:

1. _____

2. _____

3. _____

The best advice I have ever received:

_____

_____

In my life I have paid for professional help from the following people (circle):

Doctor . Lawyer . Dentist . Marriage Counselor

Financial Advisor . Architect . Success Coach

Of the previous circled professionals, whom did I consult because I was in pain or trouble?

_____

_____

Whom did I consult to proactively avoid potential trouble?

_____

_____

The date of my first appointment with a success coach is:

_____

9

Pay the Price

There are some important questions that you need to answer in analyzing your drive towards success. The first one is, "Am I willing to accept that the price of success is not fair?"

Whatever the price for success, some will pay more and some will pay less. There is no 'united workers union' that ensures a level road to success for everyone. Some will gain the things you desire with less effort. But then again, you will have an easier time than others. Some may experience a bit of luck along their path. That same luck may elude you.

The price of success is definitely not an issue of fairness. If you look too much at what someone else is paying for their progress, you may be discouraged by what you discover. If you're reading this book on a plane, you may discover that the person sitting next to you paid a lot less than you did to get to the same place! The journey to success can be like that. Some pay more; some pay less. Don't look for fairness.

The next question is, "Do I control the currency that pays the price for what I want to achieve?" For example, a friend of my son was told by a college basketball scout that if he grows another four inches, he will be assured of a full college basketball scholarship. That is an amazing amount of financial reward for growing just four more inches. A fully paid college scholarship is a great goal to have. But if the price of the scholarship has to be paid by way of inches, it is a currency which my son's friend does not control. Even if he ate all his vegetables and drank a cow's worth of milk every day, the length of his jeans is still determined by his strength of his genes.

Likewise, with being a professional opera singer. All the singing lessons in the world could not compensate for the lack of adequate vocal chords. So too with becoming the president of the United States of America. If you were not born in the United States, you are automatically disqualified from presidential candidacy. So before you embark on paying the price, make sure that the price can be paid in currency that you control. The price could be beyond your ability to pay no matter how earnest your effort.

Another question to ask is, "Am I attempting the impossible?" Yes, the world stops to applaud those who have done the impossible. Yes, it sounds heroic to 'do the impossible.' But attempting it can kick the stuffing out of your confidence if you haven't got a string of successes to uphold your confidence if things go wrong. Trying the impossible and discovering, that indeed, *it is* impossible puts you in danger of questioning your suitability for future entrepreneurial endeavors. Too many people end up squashing their entrepreneurial inclinations because they bet it all on their first big effort and lost.

Save 'doing the impossible' for later. For now, channel your exuberance wisely. Build yourself a foundation of many successes doing what *is* possible. Build, build, build success upon success.

Great achievements have a price. They never go on sale and there are three main currencies by which the price of success is paid. Everyone has these currencies at their disposal.

1. Effort

If you want it bad enough, you will put in the necessary effort. It's not about what it takes for others. It's about what it is going to take for you and whether you are willing to do what it takes. That is the bottom line.

2. Sacrifice

Unless a seed of wheat is sacrificed to the soil, there can not be a harvest. It's the law of nature and it encompasses human nature. The price of success is paid with the currency of sacrifice. For the sake of experiencing an expansive future, you put some limitations on yourself today. For example, while others are buying a new vehicle you have the courage to drive your older model for a few years longer. While others may be trading up to a bigger house, you decide to make the most of the one you have and buy a rental property instead. The money you would have spent on a new car or bigger house, you divert into strengthening your business profitability, professional advancement or property holdings.

If you sacrifice to build a portfolio of income pro-ducing assets now, in time these assets will turn you into a millionaire. Your well-applied sacrifices will produce a more positive and adventurous life in the future.

3. Overcoming Rejection

Nobody relishes being rejected. Yet it's impossible to succeed without having to experience a good deal of it. Rejection hurts but the answer lies not in avoiding it but in getting lots of it. The more you experience rejection, the less intimidated you are by it. Learn to laugh at your-self as, strangely enough, this diminishes the impact of others laughing at you.

The ability to overcome rejection is not something that you are born with. It is a skill that you develop. The only way to develop the skill is to face up to copious quantities of rejection. Decide to become adept at not taking rejection personally. Certainly increase your presen-tation skills and identify the most receptive demographics to reduce the amount of rejections. However, your goal is to continually expand your territory and that comes by way of facing new rejections. So you'll never completely eradicate rejection. It comes with the growth process. Learn to stare it down. Don't let rejection stop you. The ruts of rejection will lead you straight up to the summit of success if you keep pushing forward.

Don't be afraid to pay the price. Pay full fare. The sooner you start to pay, the sooner you will arrive at the place of enjoying your rewards.

Putting the Principle to Work

In terms of willingness to delay gratification, I would rate myself at this point on the scale:

1   10

1 - I don't sacrifice anything. If I want it, I get it now; even if I have to put it on a high interest credit card.

10 - My life is all about the future. I am a self-sacrificing misery to be around but my future is going to be amazing!

My dream is to _____

_____

Sacrificing the following things is going to help me achieve this dream sooner:

_____

_____

_____

If you are married, organize a dream date for you and your spouse. I don't mean booking into a luxury hotel for candle light dinners and spa treatments! I mean going somewhere for the purpose of talking about what you want your future to look like. Put your dreams on paper and decide what you're both willing to sacrifice in order to make the dreams come true.

10

Change the Only Person You Can

Here's a clue that will save you a million frustrations: you can not change anyone except yourself. So if your happiness depends on someone changing to suit you, be prepared to spend the rest of your life being miserable and frustrated. Your future is too precious to waste your energy on people you can't change.

Just as a motor vehicle has a fuel tank, humans have an emotional fuel tank. At any one time our supply of emotional energy is limited to what we have in our tank. Trying to change people will do little more than waste your emotional fuel, leaving you dry and lacking energy for your own life.

Let's peel back one more layer on this. Most people who feel drained by others are not actually drained by others. They are drained by their expectations of others not being fulfilled. So removing your expectations of others will save the loss of your emotional fuel.

You may be a champion in sales. You may be an inspiring motivator. You may even be a psychologist or a doctor. It doesn't matter. You can't change people. My professional colleagues and I have learned this the hard way. We have presented convincing principles and compelling logic. We discovered that if you set the emotional temperature of the room right, people will even agree with you. They might even make a verbal commitment and show promising signs of initial change. Just like moody George.

George drove into my life driving a truck fully loaded with misfortune. Upon listening to his stories, I concluded that moody George was a future champion who just needed the right change agent in his life. I decided that change agent would be me! I could succeed where all others have failed. All moody George needed was the right information and some moral support to help him institute personal change. So, countless hours were spent encouraging moody George to be brighter and more positive. I went overboard in singling him out for special input and attention.

It took me a few years to realize that moody George was doing a better job at making me moody than I was in changing him into a champion. He was not fulfilling the vision that I had for his life. And therein lay the problem. I was exhausting myself trying to change moody George into my image of him. His falling short of that image left me bewildered and frustrated. But I only had myself to blame. However noble my intentions for changing moody George, I was challenging one of the fundamental laws of humanity in doing so. People stay the same unless they will to change. The best motivational speaker in the world can not override that fact. As one of the best salesmen I know tells me, "If you convince somebody against their will, they're of the same opinion still."

You get more bang for your emotional energy buck changing yourself rather than trying to change others. If interfacing with someone is frustrating you, remind yourself that you are being frustrated by your expectations. Change yourself into a better person. Improvements to your own life actually fill your emotional tank. This will cause you to make a better impression and increases your influential capital. If you really want to help others to change, inspire them to change themselves by being a credible example of the benefits.

Putting the Principle to Work

As of (date), _____

I, _____, resign from the job of trying to change the moody George in my life.

With all the emotional energy that I get back as a result of the above resignation, I will channel that energy into the following self improvements:

1. _____

2. _____

3. _____

4. _____

5. _____

6. _____

11

Accommodate Human Diversity

How interesting would the world be if everyone were just like you? You would quickly find the world very small. In fact, if everyone were like you, you would change just to make life more interesting! So be wary of the human inclination to criticize those who don't conform to your style. Don't be threatened by human diversity. Differences are the key to enlarging your future. Instead of trying to squeeze people into your small world, engage people with the purpose to making your world larger.

Create a view of the world where you accommodate human diversity. Purposely let people be different. Unless the other party is breaking the law or posing a danger to you or others, let them be. In fact, learn 'why they be why they be!' There will be great value derived from the insight. Understanding another person's culture will do much to advance your ability to see the opportunities inherent in that culture.

You don't improve by having your opinions affirmed. You improve by having your ideas challenged. Some people feel that they will be compromising their personal values if they listen to an opposing view. Accordingly, they get uncomfortable in the presence of someone who thinks differently. Creating a world that only consists of people who agree with you is a danger to your future growth. Listening only to those who reinforce your worldview will keep your world small and you looking smaller still.

When you don't accommodate human diversity, you become narrow and judgmental by default. The world that is acceptable to you turns out to be only a fraction the size of what really exists. When you eliminate all those things that are not 'your taste or style', you have eliminated much of the world. In doing so, you confine yourself to only one section of the world's buffet of opportunities. You become a limited person and your prospects become limited. Instead of avoiding the differences, explore them. You don't have to compromise your values to learn about another's values. See what you can discover and learn. It will make you more interesting, and more attractive to others. That goes a long way to improving your value.

Remember, you are the only person that sees the world like you do. So resist the temptation to criticize others for having different perspectives. Spend your energy exploring the perspectives of others. Make it your goal to become a big world citizen not the president of your tiny self-made world. Keep a part of your life in the curious zone. Be curious about why people are different. You'll discover new fields of potential as you develop understanding. There is a lot of success and wealth that comes to those who put judgment aside and the learning cap on.

Be glad for the diversity in mankind. It is the boat off your little island if you care to embrace it and not be threatened by it.

Putting the Principle to Work

Determine to have some friends who don't share your religion, political viewpoint or ethnicity. Learn about their world without trying to defend your world to them.

My current friends who expand my world view:

1. _____

2. _____

3. _____

4. _____

5. _____

12

Spend Your Way to Millionaire

Stand back! Two myths about becoming rich are about to go up in flames. Here's the first myth: You become a millionaire by saving your money. This is false. It's virtually impossible to, dollar-by-dollar, save that much. Here's the other myth: You need a big income to become a millionaire. That is also false. There are more high school graduates becoming millionaires than medical school graduates. Crossing the millionaire line depends on your spending ability. The income that you earn is not as essential as how well you spend what you earn. Becoming a millionaire is all in your spending and how well you do it.

A well-known credit card company launched a new program that used the catch phrase "the more you spend, the more you save." To understand the premise, I will give you a scenario. Say you bought some jeans at a total cost of $89.12. The credit card company would round the expense up to $90.00 and put the additional eighty-eight cents into your savings account. Every purchase you made on the card would be rounded up to the next dollar and your savings would grow by the few cents added. It is clever marketing. People participating in the program would feel that they were spending their way to being rich. If only getting rich was that much fun. Though it is a creative idea, it is not the way to create your first million!

The rules for becoming a millionaire are quite simple. Spend as little as possible on consumables: food, drink, clothing, entertainment, cars, fashion accessories, recreational toys, and electronic gadgets. Then, spend as much as you can on wealth increasing assets: real estate, stocks, and profitable businesses.

Heading for millionaire or welfare all depends on how soon you wise up to how you spend your money. If all of your money is consumed by consumables, your chance of becoming a millionaire is consumed as well. But if you spend your money on real estate, stocks and developing profitable businesses, you will become a millionaire. No luck, sporting contract, record deal or inheritance required!

It is quite a climb to get to the millionaire level. That's the bad news. But the good news is that there is no discrimination barring your entry. Everyone is welcomed to join the millionaire club. You don't have to apply to be accepted. The standards are already set and by achieving them, you are automatically given membership into the club. Becoming a millionaire is your choice and your choice alone. Would you like to become one? Read on.

Resist the temptation to spend all your money on cars and clothes. Start budgeting and buy a home to live in as soon as you have enough money for the deposit. At first, you might be intimidated by the idea of buying real estate. That's to be expected. You are making the biggest purchase of your life to date. Find yourself a trustworthy mentor who can guide you through the process.

The location of the property is important. It's the one area in life where striving for average is better. Don't try to buy the best house on the street as you limit your potential buyers when you attempt to sell it. And until you have gained some real estate experience, don't buy the worst house on the street because you could be buying a money pit. Repairs and renovations can be frightfully expensive if you're inexperienced in the field.

Real estate should be your first goal when you start earning a real income. You need a home to live in. You can either rent one or buy one. Even though a home mortgage will cost you more per month than a rent payment, it is well worth the extra. Over time, your home will increase in value. Regardless of ups and downs, real-estate will always come back to historical norms of growth. So over the long term, most properties will double and triple in value. Many people become millionaires by this route alone. They buy and hold on to properties and let the natural capital gains process run its course. If you can resist the temptation to cash out the equity gains to buy consumables, you'll discover property growth is a powerful force in creating personal wealth.

Once you have bought your first property, start buying shares in index funds. An index fund is a mix of stocks from a selection of different companies. Don't kid yourself that you can outperform an index fund by picking a great individual stock. Unless you personally know the management of a public company, you have little idea as to how the company will perform in the future. Some people think they can find the golden needle in the haystack of public companies. Buying shares in an index fund is like buying the haystack; you buy the golden needle by default.

Now some financial advisors can prove to you that their company share fund can outperform an index fund. That may be so. But don't forget that the key to becoming a millionaire is being 'in' the market not 'out-smarting' the market. If you just keep buying more of the haystack of public companies, time will do the rest.

The taxation laws of some countries will allow you to purchase tax-advantaged funds and pay less personal income tax for doing so. Therefore, it makes good sense to spend your money this way. Over the long run, index funds can slightly outperform real estate in growth. However, you can't snuggle up to your honey on a sofa located in an index fund. On the other hand, you'll never get a phone call from your stockbroker telling you that your index fund has a leaky faucet and you need to hire a plumber to fix it. Don't get caught up in the debate over whether stocks or real estate are the better investment. Be in both. If your financial team includes both, you'll eventually win the financial championship!

If you manage your spending right, you can be on a set salary and still become a millionaire. But statistics show that more people become millionaires by owning a business than those who work jobs with set salaries. Being a business owner is an advantage, but it has to be a profitable business. Buying someone else's 'profitable' business can be a gamble. There are no guarantees that what you buy will turn out to be what you thought you were buying. Starting your own business, while maintaining your day job, is a wise way to enter the business ownership arena. As the business grows, you can ease out of your day job. The quicker it grows, the quicker you can crossover to working full time in your business.

The great thing about business ownership is that you have no ceiling on your income potential. The more you work your business, the more it works for you financially. Spend your profits to grow the business but keep buying real estate and index funds along the way. Business ownership, real estate, index funds, and some patience are all you need to become a millionaire.

When is a good age to start? Now.

Putting the Principle to Work

In the way I'm inclined to spend my money I put myself at this point on the line:

Consumables   Investments

My current net worth is $_____
                 (value of investments minus what I owe)

To increase my net worth to $ _____ by _____(date) is my goal.

I will cut back on the following consumable expenses:

1. _____

2. _____

3. _____

4. _____

5. _____

I will increase my spending on investments by _____ per week from today.

Make an appointment with a success coach to establish a wealth plan.

13

Keep a Positive Attitude

The day had been largely disappointing in what I had wanted to achieve. Nothing seemed to be going my way. Seeking to clutch at least one accomplishment from the day, I took my son, David, to get his hair cut. It was to be a small achievement in the scheme of things, but at least my son's neatened appearance would prove that the day wasn't a complete loss. Added to that, I had a coupon. I was going to save a few dollars in the process!

After the haircut, we returned to the car. As I pulled out of the parking space, the concrete-filled steel pipe that was completely obscured from my line of sight, ripped into the side of the car. I got out and viewed the damage. The steel pipe had not only left a huge indentation, it had ripped open the door panel. It looked like the car had been stabbed by a forklift.

I sat there for a few moments wondering how far my coupon savings would go to paying for the damage. Then,

I turned to David and said, "Son, your dad's not having a good day." To which he replied, "Dad, I wish I knew what I could do to make your day better." What could I say? I started the silent drive home. My son had tried to console me but I had already started my brooding slide into self-pity thinking, 'What a crummy day this has been.'

Then it hit me. Not the steel pipe this time! Reason whacked me over the head with the following thoughts: It's not my son's responsibility to make my day better, it was my responsibility. Self-pity was not going to accomplish anything other than move me from bad to worse. Brooding was not going to reverse the damage to the vehicle. I was being a poor example to my son of how to deal with misfortune.

A voice within me said, 'Do you think you have your son forever? Your times of taking your son to get his hair cut are coming to a close. Soon he will be off to college. Get yourself together and take control of your thinking. You can turn this day around simply by one decision—the decision to be positive despite what has happened.'

Having been visited by a few rational brain waves, I instantly changed from having negative thoughts to positive ones. I decided to prove my power over the situation by how I responded to it. Instead of being a bear with a sore head, I was going to be the opposite. Upon arriving home, I ran inside and made an announcement to the whole family, "Dad has smashed the car! Let's go out and celebrate with ice-cream!" And that's what we did.

A wonderful family night ensued. We ate ice cream,

told stories and laughed the night away. To think that the good time was made possible by one decision; the decision to be positive. I am reluctant to repair the damage to the car. It reminds me of the 'car smashing ice-cream celebration,' triumphing over my brooding negativity and redeeming precious moments with my son—moments that I was wastefully throwing into a mental sewer.

A positive attitude will always out-perform a negative attitude. Positive thinking will make you more friends, more money, open more doors of opportunity and elevate your life beyond what negative thinking will.

Being positive does not come easily. It will be a daily struggle and require a daily commitment and re-commitment. Every day will test you with situations that you did not expect. You will crash into things you plainly did not anticipate. Having a commitment to being positive, no matter what, is the best preparation for whatever you face.

Being positive is not a substitute for wisdom. All the positive thinking in the world will not protect you from the consequences of making dumb decisions. So, don't try and climb Mount Everest if you haven't developed the skills or done the training. There is no glory in being the most positive person who has ever perished! But if you're willing to develop your skills and train, positive thinking will get you further up the mountain than negative thinking will. Be positive. You'll be more successful for being so.

Putting the Principle to Work

The most frustrating issue in my life at the moment is:

_____

_____

_____

By the end of the day I will have diffused its negative influence by doing the following three things:

1. _____

_____

_____

2. _____

_____

_____

3. _____

_____

_____

14

Complain Only To Your Mother

Dale Carnegie wrote a timeless book called *How to Win Friends and Influence People*. In the book, he teaches the art of making friends by listening to people and being genuinely interested in what the other person is saying. The book has been famous for generations. Its powerful message has been adopted by millions and has made the world a friendlier place as a result. Dale Carnegie has long passed away but the popularity of his training classes continue to this day and are attended by thousands.

So don't be fooled next time you start complaining to someone. They may be listening to you only because Dale Carnegie has instructed them to look interested! The truth is, they really don't want to hear you complain. Your complaining irritates them. They feel their emotional energy draining away with your every passing syllable. You may think you have found a soul mate that really understands but in reality, you are lowering the listener's perception of you.

If you are going to complain, do so only to your mother because she's the only one who really cares. If someone listens to you complain once, they are being polite. Two times means you probably have them cornered. Three times and you've found a kindred spirit who will listen to you while they gather their own thoughts, waiting for their chance to complain!

The quality of your future depends very much on the quality of your connections with people. You want to be successful, so protect those connections. If someone invites you into their home, would you walk through their house with mud on your shoes? If you did, you would be leaving their home in worse shape as a result of your presence. They wouldn't invite you back. When you bring a complaining spirit into a conversation, you soil the relationship. You risk damaging the connection, possibly causing the other party to start pulling away from you. That is the last thing you want to happen, especially if they are a bridge to a better future for you.

Without doubt, you will have ample reason to complain. Everyone navigates waters fraught with perceived unfairness, injustice and inequities. It's only natural to want to vent your feelings in the wake of such. But remember no one has ever made a sale, gained a client, received a promotion or built a team by complaining. On the other hand, many people have sabotaged great opportunities by being a grumbler.

People complain because it feels good to verbally express their frustration. Although quite temporary, there are therapeutic advantages. Getting something off your chest is better than storing it inside your chest. But be conscious of the full effects. Getting something off your chest depletes the emotional energy of your listener. Unless they are a counselor being paid to listen to you, this is not a good impact to have on people.

Here's another drawback to complaining: Because complaining can make you feel a little better, you can become addicted to it for the brief therapeutic effect it provides. The complaining habit becomes intertwined with your character and presto, before you know it, you're known as a whiner!

Some people just want to complain. Avoid them and avoid becoming one of them. If issues arise that are too big for you to ignore, don't sabotage your future by 'airing your grievances.' Be solution minded in your conversations. For example, "I'm wrestling with this issue and would really value your advice on how to better deal with it" is much more constructive than, "Can you believe what was done to me? They have no idea what they're doing? How would they like it if that happened to them?"

If you are solution minded instead of complaint minded, you are going to strengthen your optimal people connections. You will increase your positive reputation and more doors of opportunity will open to you. People will talk about you with admiration. And frankly, this is the stuff your mother really wants to hear!

Putting the Principle to Work

In recognition that it has gotten me nowhere, as of this moment I am going to stop complaining about the following three things:

1. _____
2. _____
3. _____

Admitting that a certain person in your life uses you as a complaint box, determine to lovingly steer the person away from engaging you in that way from now on.

Even though it is a source of irritation to me, as of today _____ (date), I will no longer complain about the price of fuel to anyone.

15

Protect Your Assets

(Marry and Stay With the Right One)

A close second to becoming successful is staying that way. When you work so hard for what you have achieved, it makes sense to protect it from erosion. Recently I sat with a friend who is a healthy sixty years young. Always wanting to learn from those who are further along the road of life, I asked if he would give me the benefit of his financial wisdom. My opening question was, "What can I do over the next twenty years to get the best financial outcome?" His answer was not the type of financial advice I was expecting. Without a moment's hesitation he said, "Stay married!" He went on to share other points on wealth building, but staying married remained his number one tip for being wealthy.

My friend explained to me that divorce immediately cuts the value of your assets in half. Then, with divorce lawyers involved, the remaining fifty percent gets eroded even further. He was sharing from experience. My friend, along with a vast number of the population, would testify that saying goodbye to your spouse also includes saying goodbye to the bulk of your money. So as quirky as it seems, if you're going to get married, the best financial advice is to marry the right one and stay married!

Who would have thought that keeping love, romance, and respect in a marriage is the best asset protection plan around?! That being the case, here's some advice to keep you standing on solid financial ground.

Don't fall in love with someone who has been given everything. If they have never earned their own money and not learned the reality that money isn't free, run from them as fast as you can. It doesn't matter if they're the most attractive person in town. Marrying them means you are signing up to be their next personal money-dispensing machine. Money issues are the number one cause of marriage breakdown. Marrying someone with irresponsible financial expectations is disastrous. You can learn a lot about a person by their credit card use. If they maintain a high balance, reach for your running shoes.

If you are young, marry someone with a generous heart, common values and a strong work ethic. Look for someone who has either spent his or her recent years training for a vocation or establishing a river of income. Of course, it may be hard to land a person like this if you lack these qualities yourself. So increase the possibility of marrying a champion by being one.

For those a few more years down the track, a supreme start is when a guy who has already bought his first home marries a girl who has already bought her first home. In this scenario, each has learned to manage money independently. Getting married means they can live in one home and rent the other out, thus getting a great start in building wealth.

For the late bloomers, those who marry in their mature years, if either or both have significant personal assets, have a pre-nuptial agreement prepared and signed prior to walking down the aisle. As disappointing as it is, more than fifty percent of marriages end up in divorce court. For those of you who think that your love is strong, think of former Beatle, Paul McCartney. For some reason, Paul thought the magnitude of love rendered a pre-nuptial agreement unnecessary. Alas, the wealth he built over forty years is being re-distributed to people he has only known for a few years. Suffice to say, he'll be saying "I do" to a pre-nuptial agreement before saying "I do" to anyone in the future.

Of course, so much more needs to be considered in choosing a partner. This chapter is simply to remind you that marrying well and keeping your marriage strong, is the best asset protection around. The divorce tax is brutal. Make it your goal to be in the fifty percentile that avoids paying it. Just think, you can financially outperform half the population simply by staying married.

Putting the Principle to Work

(For those Married)
I currently do the following things to invest in the health of my marriage:

_____

_____

_____

If you don't already, start dating your spouse. Set aside a weekly amount in your budget to do so.

Start planning your next honeymoon. (Who says you're limited to one?)

(For those Single)
My goal is to bring the following assets to a marriage:

_____

_____

_____

_____

_____

16

Focus on Achievement
Not Discipline

Too many people are hard on themselves because of their perceived 'lack of discipline.' How many times have you quietly harangued yourself by saying, "I need to be more disciplined" or berated yourself with the comment, "If only I was more disciplined." Much of our dissatisfaction in life can be solved, we think, with more personal discipline. Do you have to be the epitome of self-discipline in order to be successful?

One day, I had a burst of personal inspiration and decided it was my time to really get disciplined. It was such an epiphany that I didn't want my family to miss out on the benefits. So I announced that as a family we were going to become more disciplined. I sat down and mapped out a daily schedule that had every moment planned. Every activity was compartmentalized into a block of time during the day. We would stay focused. The schedule would keep us on track. Not a minute was going to be frittered away frivolously.

Once the 'super-schedule' was mapped out, I printed it and gave copies to all of the parties involved. From that point on, we knew exactly how each day would unfold. At these times, we worked. At this time, we took a break. At these designated times, we were to stop for meals. Wow, I was excited. We were on our way to becoming one incredible production machine, thanks to being disciplined. I had finally cracked the code. Look out world!

How long did it last? One day. At least, for me. To my family's credit, they managed to string a few days together before we all settled back into our normal lifestyle. What was it about this 'super-schedule' attempt at discipline that didn't work? Was I incapable of being highly structured? Did I provide bad leadership? Was I unwilling to commit to labor and process? Was I a lazy, no good sloth? A mental check of my financial assets balance sheet quickly proved that if I was a sloth, then I had managed to become a wealthy one!

Some people are extremely disciplined. They thrive on structure and regiment. They would be selected to compete in the Discipline Olympics. Yet, others can be free spirited and still grow a high net worth. So there must be more to it. And there is.

If discipline were the key to success, then the army would be the greatest producer of future millionaires.

But that is not so. While discipline is important in the scheme of things, trying to become 'more disciplined' is a waste of emotional energy. Thinking that you need to become more disciplined does little more than grind down your self-esteem. You end up reinforcing a sense of being personally inadequate because you 'lack self-discipline.' Striving to be more disciplined is the wrong focus. The key to success is to focus less on becoming disciplined and focus more on achievement.

Achievement is the goal of every successful person. You may have all the self-discipline in the world but still not achieve anything. Achievement should be your objective. Focus your efforts on what you want to achieve, then discipline will show up automatically.

Your problem is never a lack of self-discipline. If you can't get out of bed, it's not due to lack of self-discipline. If you procrastinate, it's not due to a lack of self-discipline. If you over-eat, it's not due to a lack of self-discipline. It comes down to what you want to achieve. If you want to achieve something badly enough, then the discipline needed to achieve it will naturally start to flow. So never berate yourself for lacking self-discipline. Instead, unmercifully berate yourself for not wanting to achieve anything thrilling enough to inspire self-discipline! Self-discipline will start to flow naturally when you become passionate about achieving something.

Putting the Principle to Work

Make a list of ten things you want to achieve on the left. Next to each rate your level of passion for achieving it (scale one to ten). On the right side rearrange the order of your list according to the level of passion you have. Apply yourself to that which is now on the top of your list, the one thing for which you have the most enthusiasm. Achieving the first on the list will add fuel to you achieving the rest.

Things I Want to Achieve	Passion Rating	Things I Want to Achieve in Order of Passion
1. _____	_____	1. _____
2. _____	_____	2. _____
3. _____	_____	3. _____
4. _____	_____	4. _____
5. _____	_____	5. _____
6. _____	_____	6. _____
7. _____	_____	7. _____
8. _____	_____	8. _____
9. _____	_____	9. _____
10. _____	_____	10. _____

17

Earn a Credential

"So, what do you do?" It's often the first question asked when two people meet for the first time. If you haven't been asked this question a hundred times, you will be. People want to know how you fit into the world. We live in a culture that wants to get a handle on you and quickly. Like it or not, we are being categorized and classified all the time. I would love to say that you are unconditionally loved for who you are and not for what you do. But everyone, other than God and your parents, are going to value you on what you've achieved. That's just the way that it is. So when you are asked, "What do you do?" make no mistake about it, you are being interviewed. In such moments, it's time to flash your credential. Your value in their eyes is about to be decided.

What is the most impressive thing about you? That is your credential. When you are starting out in life, the best thing you can do is earn a credential. The most obvious one is to gain some educational qualification. Someone who has some advanced education has a greater credential than someone without. Yet you don't need to go to college for a great credential. Someone who loves to travel can earn an impressive credential. Imagine saying, "I have a Bachelor's Degree in Adventure." If you have traveled to forty different nations of the world, you have earned one. It is a credential worth talking about and probably cheaper than a typical college degree!

Relationships are the bridges to future opportunity. If you have relationships with successful people better opportunities will grow out of these relationships. Good credentials are the key to establishing relationships with successful people. The better your credential, the better will be your impression.

If you haven't done anything interesting, then do something worth talking about. If you have not got an impressive credential, set about gaining yourself one. This is not about you bragging or nauseating someone with a list of your great qualities. This is simply about you helping the other person establish a positive perception of you. They are going to determine their impression of you anyway. Why don't you give them some great material to work with?

Being a business owner is a solid credential with great impression potential. Starting and running a community non-profit organization is another. Getting a motorcycle license and riding a Harley Davidson is a door-opening credential to a certain demographic. I have a friend who is the flight captain of a Falcon jet for a private group of investors. That sure impresses me. How did he get that credential? He got his pilot's license and progressively built on it.

I have another friend whose company designs famous landmarks. Whenever I introduce him, I say, "I'd like you to meet my friend, who designed that famous California landmark." While my friend has heard me introduce him countless times that way, he understands that I am simply using his particular credential to help others to connect with him.

When you have a credential, you make it easier for people to introduce you to their circles. Whatever time you spend on securing a credential will be paid back to you. Armed with some type of credential, you will cover more territory faster than you would without one. So go to the trouble of achieving something interesting and noteworthy. It is a great way to open doors to significant relationships.

Picture yourself having just been seated on an airplane next to a very influential person. If after the plane has taken off and dinner and drinks have been served, the influential person turns to you and asks, "So tell me what do you do?", what will you tell them?

Putting the Principle to Work

The most impressive thing about me would be:

_____

_____

_____

My top three credentials would be:

1. _____

2. _____

3. _____

Acknowledging that having personal interests makes me more interesting to others, I will seek to gain credentials in the following areas:

_____

_____

_____

18

Gather Your Success
Along the Way

We like the David versus Goliath stories. We like to hear about the little guy who, against all odds, defeats the big intimidating behemoth. These stories give us hope that it's possible to have one big breakthrough that changes everything. When it comes to our financial lives, we love the idea that one big victory can create enough success to eliminate all our financial challenges. And we should love the idea. Big economic breakthroughs still happen every day and they can happen to you. So, go for the big breakthrough. Keep pursuing it. But be smart in the way you do it. In your pursuit of a big victory, don't devalue the power of your smaller, seemingly insignificant successes along the way. Insignificant profits can play a powerful role in helping you succeed financially.

Too many people consume their little profits in hot pursuit of the 'big one' that will solve all their fiscal woes. This is okay if you eventually bag the big one, but it is traumatic if you run out of energy before then. Many dynamos have wound up exhausted with nothing to show for it but an empty bag. The smart person doesn't over-look his small profits even when they don't look like much. He uses the power of accumulation to his advantage. He realizes that, left in isolation, small profits are negligible but gathered together they become economically potent. Small profits collected can equal the value of a big pay off.

If you become skilled at gathering your small profits, you will become successful regardless of whether you land the big payoff or not. The skill of gathering your small profits will fortify your potential for landing the bigger profits as well. When you gather your profits, you gather momentum by default. And momentum is a valuable asset in your pursuit of the 'big one'.

An ounce of gold is still an ounce of gold regardless of whether it comes in a coin or in little fragments. So too, success is success whatever format it comes in; whether you earned it in one big deal or gathered it up via many little deals. It's easier to fight on when you have some gold in the hold rather than just a bag full of hope.

Many successful people can't point to any massive breakthrough to which they attribute their financial strength. They just quietly set about combining their blessings no matter how small their size. Every little bit counted and, added with other little bits, became a compounding force that continued to grow.

Be bold in your goals but don't forget to gather up your little pieces of profit along the way. A small profit can buy you a nice dinner. But small profits gathered together can buy you a house. Until you get your 'one big breakthrough' that causes a media frenzy, gather your little pieces and leverage them to your advantage and advancement. This will do wonders for your confidence and likely put you in a place of never needing the 'big breakthrough'.

Putting the Principle to Work

Establish a Gathering Fund. Start by gathering up all the loose change and money lying around in various locations with no purpose. Close bank accounts that are no longer used. Identify valuable things no longer needed and sell them. Set yourself the goal of raising $_____ just by assembling all your little pieces.

Determine that from today onwards, _____% of every future profit will be set aside into the Gathering Fund.

Establish a meaningful and inspiring purpose for the Gathering Fund. Write your purpose for the Gathering Fund here.

_____

_____

_____

19

Produce Bankable Results

(Get the Real Work Done)

If being busy were the key to success, this book would be called Go and Be Busy. In reality, being busy can be a major diversion from success. So watch out for it. Be careful that you don't get sidetracked with being busy. Being 'busy' is not a sign of success. It could well be a sign of the opposite. If you scratch beneath the surface of most people's 'busyness', you will often find that their hectic work is not producing much at all. Some people even use busyness as a way to avoid productivity. You can so easily fill up your schedule up with work and fool people into thinking you're a champion. What's worse, you can even fool yourself into thinking you must be a champion because you are always working. Here is the bottom line: If your work is not producing bankable results, you are not working. You are just being active.

This chapter may be uncomfortable for you to read. It could be pulling back the covers on your cover-up. You have been scurrying around the place giving the right impression that you are hard at it. To support the good impression, you report to your work colleagues a list of activities in which you have been 'heavily engaged.' But deep down you know you're not accomplishing much. The busy impression is really a smoke screen that you hope blinds people from noticing your empty bank account. There's no joy in being busy and broke.

If you are engaged in the business of selling goods or services, be especially mindful of what is keeping you occupied. Your demanding schedule could be a thief in disguise, robbing you of future income. When you are in the business of selling goods or services, the real work is what puts money in the bank. That's the bottom line. Real productivity produces prosperity.

For years, I have seen artists, musicians, and authors develop their craft and even produce 'products' that people can buy. They think that the work is producing the song, writing the book or painting the canvas. They could not be further from the truth. The real work is marketing the product and selling the product. Too many talented people end up with a pallet-load of product stored in their garages. They have either exhausted themselves producing the product or they have 'call reluctance' in marketing and selling the product. If I only had a dollar for every author that has said to me, "I love writing but I'm just not comfortable doing the marketing and selling. I prefer to let someone else take care of that." Reality check! Writing the book, recording the album, inventing the widget, producing the presentation folio is the fun part. The real work begins when you go to sell it.

The world belongs to the person not with the best product, but the person with the courage and tenacity to sell the product he has. There are brilliant products sitting in garages and warehouses around the world. But the product's value is only unlocked when the consumer pays money for it. The real hero in the process is the one who gets the product into the hands of the buyer.

Economic advisor Paul Zane Pilzer says it this way, "While accountants record inventory on a company's balance sheet as a physical asset, inventory has no real economic value—inventory consists of products or services that someone has worked hard to produce but are not needed yet. Distributors add so much value in our economy because they find the end users who turn inventory into consumption."

So you can have a valuable product. That's good. You can have the neatest warehouse in the world. That's great. Your products can be efficiently categorized, sorted and stacked. Well done. You can have the most impressive sales brochures and media presentations. Excellent. You can have the latest phone with all the features. But until you pick up that phone, call a prospect and make a sale, you haven't done any work worth talking about.

Putting the Principle to Work

Evaluate your day and conclude the following: _____%
of my activity actually puts money in the bank.

I will cut back on the following activities to focus more on
real productivity:

1. _____

2. _____

3. _____

I will increase my activity in the following areas to increase
what I am putting in the bank:

1. _____

2. _____

3. _____

List your tasks for each day. On the top of the page write
the words: *There is no joy in being busy and broke. Get the real
work done. . . first!*

20

Let Time Make You Rich

Set aside the belief that money makes you rich. It's time that makes you rich. If you invest a little money in the right place, time will turn it into a much larger sum. Young people are wise to purchase investments as soon as they can. Start young and you will have the benefit of time producing great wealth for you. But, whatever your age, it's never too late to start investing. This is your time to let time make you wealthy.

The first car I ever bought was a Leyland Marina. It cost me two thousand dollars. I thought it was a cool car until I read a review in *Wheels Magazine*, that said "it handles well at parking speeds!" Nonetheless, it was my pride and joy and the most significant purchase of my life up to that point. A few years later, I bought a one-bedroom apartment with a three thousand dollar deposit. It seemed like a crazy purchase at the time. The property wasn't even located in the city where I was living. I put the property in the hands of a real estate property manager. They kept the place rented to a tenant in return for a commission on the rental income. When the first tenant left, the property manager advertised and found another tenant.

Year after year, the one bedroom investment plodded along with tenants coming and going. Even property managers would hand it off to new property managers. Sometimes even the property management company would be sold to another management company. In total, I kept the property for twenty years without ever spending one night in it. At the time of selling the property, the rental income had increased by a modest 65%. Not very impressive by investment standards. Yet, when I ended up selling the property, the value of it had increased a whopping seven hundred percent from the purchase price. And better than that, the actual return on my initial three thousand dollar investment was immensely more than seven hundred percent.

Each year, the rental income basically covered the costs associated with owning the property. The downside of the rental income was that none of it went into my pocket. The upside of the rental income was that it stopped the apartment from taking money out of my pocket. It wasn't costing me anything to hold onto the property for as long as I wanted. The rental arrangement was buying me time and time was performing its magic. My profit was not in the monthly rental income but rather in the way the property increased in value over the years.

Looking back, I made two large purchases around

that time of my life: the Leyland Marina car and the one-bedroom apartment. I invested close to the same amount of money into both. The Leyland Marina's value diminished and was eventually sent to the scrap heap. It has no continuing value except the memory of a few good road trips and one bad accident. But the one-bedroom apartment kept improving in value. When I sold the apartment, the profits went straight into another investment property. So every dollar that was once in the one bedroom apartment, continues to live on and grow within the life of the new investment property. I am not doing much except making a few responsible decisions and being patient. Time is doing the bulk of the work. Time is working for me and it wants to work for you as well.

Time does not favor one person over another. It will work equally as hard for you as it will for another. All it asks is that you give it a little something to work with. So scrape together whatever funds you can and buy a prudent investment. If you do, time will work for you as your partner in wealth creation. Deny time any investments to work with and time will work against you. The more investments you give to time, the harder time will work for you. While you are sleeping, time will be working to increase the value of your investments. When you are on vacation, time will stay at work. Time never takes time off. It's the most loyal business partner you will ever have.

Putting the Principle to Work

Time is increasing my personal wealth as the result of the following investments:

_____

_____

_____

_____

If you own property, invite an agent to come and appraise its value. Let them know up front that you are not wanting to sell but that you just want an idea of the property value. Often real estate agents will be happy to do so, just to build a relationship with you. Once you have the valuation, compare your purchase price to its current value. Determine the average annual increase to your net worth.

Purchase Price _____

Current Value _____

Difference _____

Years owned _____

Increase to net worth each year _____

If you don't own a property, buy one. But find a success coach who can advise you how to best become a property owner and help to steer you through the process.

21

Achieve Financial Independence

Make it your goal to become financially independent. There are some good governments in the world but you would be unwise to depend on them for your future welfare. There are some great jobs and bosses in the world but it's too risky to look to them for financial security. Industries, organizations and corporations are not stable enough to guarantee an income forever.

Generations ago, you could be employed for your entire working life by one company. In turn, the company would show appreciation for your loyalty by continuing to pay you long after you've stopped working for them. This was called a retirement package with defined benefits. But times have changed and things like job security and company backed retirement packages have mostly disappeared. In short, each one of us is now responsible for our own financial security.

There are market forces, government policies and

population shifts that have caused this change in who is responsible for your welfare. Without going into the historical and political background, suffice to say, you are now on your own baby! Unless you want to pack up and move to one of the remaining communist nations, your future financial strength is totally up to you. The government will do its best, but its best will be nowhere near what you will need in order to live. As *Fortune Magazine's* Nina Easton says, "In the new economy, we all have to be entrepreneurs with our own lives—with all the rewards and risks."

This change has been taking effect for some years. Yet people have not taken the message seriously. At the current rate, if you take ten people in their retirement years, one will be financially independent and well able to enjoy continual income from investments, four will be just 'getting by', and the remaining five will be working jobs for the rest of their lives or dependent on others.

Everyone has the potential to become financially independent. But you have to make it your personal goal. It's not going to happen by accident. Man didn't land on the moon because he just happened to be flying near it that day. It required years of planning and preparation. But unlike flying to the moon, you don't have to be a rocket scientist to reach financial independence. Anyone can be that one person in ten who achieves financial freedom. You just need to work a viable plan.

Financial freedom is that point where you have a river of money flowing into your life that is not dependent on your personal exertion. In effect, the river of money continues to flow without you having to work to make it flow. This is called residual or passive income. It comes from investment properties, stock dividends, interest payments, royalties, and business ownership distributions.

So how do you create this never-ending river of money that will allow you to stop working if you so desire? Use the first part of your life working to create the river. The sooner you get started the better.

The temptation for young people is to procrastinate. They agree that building a river of residual income is a good idea, but they also feel that they have time on their side. So they wait until later before starting to build their river. Procrastinating is risky. You end up establishing a spending lifestyle that doesn't incorporate any efforts towards river building. Starting 'later on' is harder because you have to break the comfortable habit of spending all your money on consumables. That's a hard habit to break.

The longer your river has been in existence, the more capacity it has to produce a big economic yield. A money river that has years of compounding momentum can provide you with powerful economic energy. The twenty year old that starts her river with trickle investing will always outperform the forty year old who has to pour large amounts of his income into a non-existent river to get the flow started.

The basic principle is this: Work now to build your financial river and that river will keep you financially buoyant for the rest of your days.

As a success counselor, the most heart-wrenching counseling sessions I have are with people who have reached their latter years without having created a river of residual income. By that stage, their options are limited. Sometimes the government will let them sail on the government's river. But the government's river is crowded and boring.

Spend the first years of your income producing life working hard to build a river of residual income. Then you can spend the rest of your years with far greater freedom to live the way you desire. So work, work, work and get that river of residual income flowing. The sooner you start the better. But better late than never!

Work is a hard concept to sell. The pitch to make big money quickly without much effort is an easier sell. I could cleverly package the wealth-building message to sound easy and fun. It may help me sell books but it's not going to help you achieve financial independence. Better for you to know the hard facts, find your peace with them, and then set about applying yourself to making the facts work for you. I could tell you that you don't need to work hard, that you just need to work smart. In full conscience, I must tell you the truth. You need to work both hard *and* smart. Reading this book is smart. Applying its principles is the work part.

Keep in mind that work is not the enemy. Work is actually good for the human spirit. Work keeps people alive. The enemy is having no autonomy. Having no freedom to decide whether you will work and for how long if you do. That's the real enemy—no freedom for self-determination when it comes to personal exertion. Reaching financial independence means you engage in work on your terms, not terms thrust upon you.

If procrastination in starting the river is the danger for young people, the danger for those older in years is thinking that it's too late to start building a river. Obviously, it's more advantageous to start earlier but you are never too old to start the river of enduring income. You may have to play some serious catch up to get a sizeable flow but there is another point to consider. It's exciting to see residual income start flowing into your life regardless of the amount. So get your river going! Experience the thrill of being paid from investments working for you.

Having more money is not the main purpose of achieving financial independence. It's having the freedom that financial independence brings. You have no say in getting older. But financial freedom allows you to say what older looks like. Achieving financial independence is a big key to a larger, more meaningful life. So get that river started!

Putting the Principle to Work

If I were to stop personal exertion today, $ _____ per week would continue to flow into my life.

_____% of my living expenses would be covered by my river of residual income.

Make an appointment with a success coach and establish a plan for increasing your residual river and achieving financial independence.

22

Fight Smart

To succeed, you have to call upon the fighter within you. The prize lies on the other side of the battlefield. You have to fight a formidable army of mindsets, traditions, cultures, perceptions, attitudes, ignorance, and bigotry. You can't be passive. If you want to see success in your life, then be prepared to armor up for the battle. There will be inevitable resistance to your advancement. You can't shrink back in the hope that you will somehow win the prize anyway. So, a fighter you must be. But it's not as simple as putting on your mental boxing gloves. Being combat ready is not an issue of just being a trained fighter. It's an issue of fighting smart. Surprisingly, fighting smart will mean that you will fight less, not more. Here's why.

Too many times, we go into battle over issues that are irrelevant to the prize for which we are striving. And that is a foolish fight. A smart fighter will always check the relevance of the battle to the prize. You don't have to win every battle in order to win the war. In fact, someone who enters every battle can be in great danger of losing the war. If the battle bears no consequence to winning the war, then it has depleted you of precious energy supplies. It has diverted you from your ultimate objective. So you must pick your battles.

The best way to pick your battles is to ask this question: "What is it that I am fighting for?" Too easily our view of the prize gets lost amidst the pile of life's issues. How many times have you gone a few rounds with a foe only to realize later that it has left you drained and for no good reason? There is no benefit engaging in a fight that gets you no closer to your goal. Even if you win the fight, the preservation of your pride is no compensation for the energy you have lost and the delay it causes.

The prize is your reference point. The line between where you are now and where you want to be will be dotted with many points of contention. But you don't have to participate in every one of them. You must ask yourself the question: "Does the outcome of this confrontation help me get closer to the life that I aspire?" Answering this question will be easier if you have an unshakable vision of what you are working towards. Often people end up engaging in nit-picking confrontations because they don't have a cause compelling enough to give them reason to avoid them.

Not every foe is in the way of your flight path. Many times, foes are simply in your airspace. They're not actually impeding your progress. If you keep your focus on your destination, you can move forward largely unaffected. However, if you take your eyes off your destination, the irritation of your foes will tempt you to engage them just to set them straight! So, engage them not. Doing so will deplete you of energy and delay your arrival.

There will be times when you must stand your ground and fight. But not every fight is worth engaging. If a confrontation has no relevance to your goal, have the courage to walk away. Doing so will preserve your energy for moving closer towards you goal. Oftentimes, fighting smart means not fighting at all.

Putting the Principle to Work

I hereby choose not fight the following battles. Even if I win them, they have no positive impact upon me reaching my goals.

1. _____

2. _____

3. _____

4. _____

5. _____

23

Safeguard Your Confidence

Never, never, never give up. Is success really as simple as following this advice? It sounds heroic and noble. Is it the ultimate key to success?

This is the most challenging chapter for me to write. On the one hand, I know that success does not come easily. You have to believe in yourself. You have to take risks. You have to face and overcome many obstacles. You have to keep going when most others would quit. You plainly cannot succeed if you have a propensity to give up when the going gets hard. Too many times, I have seen people give up when they could have succeeded with more effort and patience. I believe in persevering because it has paid off time and time again in my life.

Yet, on the other hand, I also know that if you are heading down the wrong track, persevering will cause you to become miserable and ineffective. Consider the famous cliché, "Winners never quit and quitters never win!"

Somebody humorously added, "But those who never quit even when they never win are idiots!" Though tongue in cheek, there is an element of truth in what they have added. There is a great danger in never winning. Too much time and effort without any positive results will devastate your confidence. This can leave you not just downhearted, but virtually crippled of any sense of self worth. It's a terrible thing to go through life without confidence. You end up questioning everything about your existence and usually come to the wrong conclusions about your value.

I want to be an advocate for 'never giving up' but if it's going to lead you down the road to further despair, I am giving you the wrong advice. Success breeds more success. So with whatever you set your mind to achieving, you need to have at least some success; enough success to give you the sense that what you are doing is working. The issue for you is not breaking a world record but rather having enough success to ward off the breaking of your heart.

There comes a time when you have to assess your efforts against the results. If you are exhausting yourself without one single breakthrough, you need to make the following assessments:

1. Has it been done by others like you?

A standard business practice is to compare apples with apples and oranges with oranges. Knowing that others have achieved what you aspire to achieve is not necessarily an indication that you can do it, too. You might be an apple when they are an orange. They may possess factors that you simply do not have and may never have. Trying to be inspired by someone else's success may lead you further down the road of frustration. If you lack certain traits that are integral to the other person succeeding, you are setting yourself up for failure by thinking that you can do the same.

If you are not succeeding, look around for a person similar to you who has succeeded. If you are a bit of a nervous Nelly, look for another nervous Nelly who has been able to succeed despite her nervousness. For if you find her, she is your living proof that you can do it too. Accordingly, learn from her. But if you are the only nervous Nelly in a field filled with confident Cathy's, then you may have to consider whether it's realistic to expect to win whilst remaining a nervous Nelly.

2. Are there skills required which you have not developed?

Sometimes you can be on the right track but just lack the skills to move you into the winner's circle. It often takes more than a dream to succeed. All the passion in the world may not be enough to overcome your need for certain skills. Ask those who have succeeded what skills helped them the most. Set yourself about the task of developing those skills. It is always possible that a nervous Nelly can become a confident Cathy by learning some new skills.

3. Are you fishing in the right pond?

If the person standing next to you is catching fish and you are not, investigate what bait they are using. But if you are the only person fishing in that pond, there may be a good reason for it. You could be fishing in the wrong pond. Remember, success is a confidence game. The more confidence you have, the more success you will attract. You need to be realizing some profit otherwise your confidence will take a dive dragging your future with it.

Continuing to fish in the wrong spot is not a testimony to your perseverance. It could very well be an indication of your stubbornness and lack of wisdom. Ask advice from those who have succeeded. There is no valor in persevering if it's leading you down the road to depression. Too many people throw away their confidence because they are too proud to admit that they made an error in judgment.

4. Are there other ways to reach the same destination?

Rarely does the 'one right way' rule apply on the road to success. While we can learn much from those who have gone before us, conditions may change requiring us to alter our approach. It's no use keeping your shoulder to the wheel if the wheel isn't moving and has not been moving for a while. There's often more than one way to get to any desired destination. If you're stuck, stop pushing and grunting. Start thinking and asking.

Every time it rained, my front yard would flood. It puzzled me because there was an underground drainage pipe that was meant to carry the excess water from the yard out to the road. The tiny trickle of water from the drainage pipe onto the street compared to the amount of water backed up at the collection point led me to assume that there must have been some blockage in the pipe.

After practically digging a crater in the front yard, I discovered that the blockage was in the section of pipe that was beneath a concrete sidewalk. So I decided to replace the section of pipe under the sidewalk. But how? I didn't want to cut through the concrete. I thus set myself the task of digging a cavity underneath the sidewalk through the hardened clay. It was like digging out of a concrete prison cell with a teaspoon.

Frustrated, I called a friend who had some experience with plumbing. He told me to put a small nozzle on my garden hose, turn on the water and use the pressurized water stream to 'blast' a channel underneath the sidewalk. It worked brilliantly. After an hour of trying to dig my way through the hard clay with a hand shovel and getting nowhere, the water jet blasted a hole from underneath one side of the sidewalk through to the other in a few painless minutes.

Let me reiterate. If you're stuck, stop pushing and grunting. Start thinking and asking.

5. What is working in your life?

One of the most pertinent pieces of advice given to me during a challenging time was this, "Go where you are celebrated, not where you are tolerated." In other words, align your efforts with the flow of favor. Ask yourself what has worked in your life and flow in that direction. Be more selective in where you put your efforts. Pick your battles. Stack the odds in your favor by going to where you experience the most favorable responses. Not every giant is worth fighting. Fight the giants who are standing at a place where you feel strong and competent.

6. Do you have the wrong people surrounding you?

I have a dear friend who regularly leaves her home in the United States bound for Thailand. There she teaches the English language to classrooms of forty children at a time. Not bad for a woman aged eighty-three! Recently, as my wife and I were taking her to the airport for another teaching stint in Thailand, I asked her the secret to her youthfulness. She simply replied, "I don't hang around old people. All they talk about is their ailments, this sickness, that sickness, this doctor, that medication. I just try to avoid old people lest I become one of them!"

One of the great wonders of humanity is how we are so deeply influenced by the people with whom we associate. If you want to determine the quality of your future, look at the quality of the people with whom you connect with at the moment. If you are struggling for a breakthrough, it could be the result of being under the influence of the wrong people.

Being socially accepted by all the wrong people is never a good substitute for winning in life. To win, you need to get more of the right people in your life. You may not be able to eliminate all the negative voices in your life but proactively surrounding yourself with positive people is akin to installing personal mock absorbers. The presence of upbeat people will always help you ride out the bumps caused by other people mocking you.

One of the keys to being successful is safeguarding your confidence. This is not to say you should play it safe or attempt only that for which success is guaranteed. True success demands that you take risks and persevere in the face of significant challenges. Safeguarding your confidence is all about protecting that vital element that keeps you strong in the face of great challenge and ultimately helps you to succeed. Don't throw away your confidence by persisting with behavior that relentlessly fails to deliver any encouraging results in a realistic time frame.

John Chen is the Chairman and CEO of the Sybase Corporation. He has made a career of coming into companies that are down and returning them to profitability. He has a three-step process: The first step is to re-instill confidence, the second step is to achieve survival status, and the third step is to work on winning. So powerful is the confidence factor that John Chen addresses that before even working on survival. He knows that confidence has to precede survival.

Have you lost your confidence? Did you unload it somewhere? Have you unconsciously thrown your confidence away? You can get it back. Return to the place where you last felt confident and start again from there. Attend inspiring conferences. Change the lineup of people that you hang around. Do whatever you need to do to get some wins back on your scoreboard. Your confidence can come back just as quickly as it was lost. And when you get it back, safeguard it!

Putting the Principle to Work

Doing the following makes me feel like I am operating in my strengths. I feel confident performing these tasks:

_____

_____

_____

_____

Doing the following erodes my self-confidence:

_____

_____

_____

Evaluate each task that leaves you drained and erodes your self-confidence and ask the following questions:

Has it been done by others like me?

Are there skills required which I haven't developed?

Am I fishing in the right pond?

Is there another way to reach the same destination?

Am I surrounding myself with the wrong people?

24

Outwork Your Competition

Let me say a word in praise of hard work. It still works. Hard work still makes people rich! Yet it has become a forgotten factor in producing success. For many years, the mantra in the marketplace has been, "Don't work hard, work smart." Everyone signed on to the mantra and understandably so. Who wants to work hard when you can be paid just as much for working smart instead? So hard work as a success philosophy has somewhat paled into the background of relevancy. In fact, too much personal exertion has come to mean that you are not working smart.

The 'work smart not hard' principle was a call for people to use their heads when approaching labor. For instance, let's say you have tremendous client skills. When put fully to work, your skills result in increased sales and revenue. Yet your face-to-face time with clients is being limited by having to leave the field in order to do paperwork back at the office. Working smart means evaluating the cost of hiring someone to do the paperwork freeing you to generate more clients. Working smart means you are constantly evaluating the relevance of what you do in relation to getting the best return for your effort. Using your brain can lead you to a place of not having to lift a finger or break a sweat. But if you are really smart, you'll do both—work smart and break a sweat.

This is not a call for you to become a workaholic. It is not a call for you to become someone who can't relax. There are one hundred and sixty eight hours in a week. If you work hard for sixty hours a week, it still leaves you with over one hundred hours for other activities. Work hard so that you can enjoy more in the future. Those that maximize their working week will eventually have all one hundred and sixty eight hours of their week to do as they please.

My son played basketball on a 'twelve and under' basketball team. Zack was the smallest kid on the team yet he had more court time than his teammates. It was not because he was the highest scorer or the best rebounder. He simply raised the level of action on the court. He learned early in the season that he couldn't out-muscle most of the other players. But Zack also figured out that he could out-hustle them. That's the secret to success: Being willing to get out there and hustle. What you lack in natural talent, you can make up for with sheer effort.

Many people busy themselves being clever and inventive. Sometimes, someone comes up with a brilliant idea that rockets the founder to fame and fortune. It's great to live in a world where that's still possible. But you don't need to be clever and inventive in order to be successful. There are many great innovations, systems and organizations already in place. Commit to one and establish your value by working hard. The world makes way for someone whose effort delivers increasing volume and revenue. If at all possible, engage yourself in enterprise that financially rewards extra effort—an enterprise with a bonus program so that the more effort you give, the more you get rewarded.

A good friend of mine tells his sales team, "I've got good news and bad news. The bad news is there's a lot of competition out there. The good news is the competition isn't that good!" You can outwork your competition by being someone who is willing to start earlier and work later, travel further, learn more, and ask for more responsibility. In a world that defines 'fulltime work' as being around thirty-five to forty hours a week, it's not hard to go the extra mile. It has never been easier to gain the reputation for being a valued, hard worker.

There's a saying out in the marketplace, "Good help is hard to find." Through the ages, that has always been the case. It always will be. People with a strong work ethic are valuable and will always stand out from the pack.

Putting the Principle to Work

Find out who led the field in sales and sign-ups last month. Beat them. I don't mean with a club! Beat their results!!

This person led the field last month:

_____

Each workday this month, get up thirty minutes earlier. Invest the time in increasing your revenue. Go to bed thirty minutes earlier if you have to.

I will arise at this time: _____

I will go to bed at this time: _____

For the purpose of increasing my revenue, I will do the following with the extra time:

_____

_____

_____

_____

_____

25

Start Now

Some people are exceptionally talented. The artist and songwriter Sting would be one of them. It would be easy to attribute his success to his talent. Undeniably, Sting's natural ability has played a huge role in getting him where he is today. Yet to think that he has ridden on the back of natural ability alone would be wrong. On his website, Sting posts, "I'm not one of these guys who waits around for inspiration. I don't sit in the lotus position and meditate and hopefully I'll channel some God-given message. What I actually do is I put the hours in. I work. I actually practice music."

Sting could easily rest and be carried by his success. Yet for some reason, he has a commitment to continue working at his craft. He's proactive. Rather than waiting for inspiration to strike, Sting goes out in search of it. He has a 'get up and at it' spirit. That spirit drove his talent into the game. Without that spirit, it is most likely that

Sting and his immense talent would still be sitting on the sidelines.

Drive is the key. Your level of natural ability may not be up to you, but your level of drive is. You have control of your drive mechanism. Drive is your choice. The person with less talent and more drive will always out-perform the one who has more talent and no drive.

This book was written to motivate you to get up and at it. When are you going to do that? Tomorrow? The inspiration might have worn off by then. Start now. Get up and at it. You've got what it takes. Go and be successful.

—Wes Beavis